# GOD IS REAL

*There are so many things that God wants you to know as his child (of God).*

*God uses different people and their experiences to let you know he does exist; he wants a relationship with you! I am no different than you in his eyes, he loves you just as much as he loves me. He is just using me as a messenger, because I agreed to write and gave myself to him. We have free will and I told God he can use me as he wants, as I am here to serve him as my father and creator.*

1

*Dear Reader:*

*ESPECIALLY FOR YOU:*

*I am writing my book as a letter especially for you, so as you read this book please think of me as if I am talking to you in a letter, as you were meant to read my book. I am so excited to share everything I know and tell you about my personal near death experience.  My story may be a little different than others.  I do believe that everyone does not experience the exact same thing.  I believe that God has a purpose for each of us and our experiences are to be uniquely different.*

*As a child brought up in a broken home environment, my mom and biological father divorced when I was about 5 or 6.  I remember some unstable times with my Mother and her raising me; she however did the best I believe she knew how.  She was a good mom and loved her children without a doubt; she was a very hard worker to support us for sure. However she seemed to drink all the time and her life was centered around alcohol, and too much for my liking. It was her decision to divorce my father. She had her own reasons I suppose as to why she did not want to be with him. I know my father had hit her at times, as to why, I don't know. In my eyes though, no women should be hit or beaten or threatened verbally abused at any time. One time, I remember them fighting with me in between them and that was the last I saw them together. I remember my dad trying to make my mom stay and saying he would change. I think my mom kept some things from us children to protect us.*

*My mom clearly wanted a different life, but I think often felt guilty for wanting one. She jumped the fence probably not exactly the way she should have but was striving for that better life. Funny thing about my (real) father is that all I remember of him is him slapping my thumb out of my mouth and making me cry, and at Christmas one year throwing me over his shoulders and running me down the stairs because Santa was here and I could hear a ho ho ho. My cousin - Sheri and I were so excited - lol. I remember my mom and dad singing and mom playing the organ around Christmas, and all of the kids would join in singing jingle bells. My parents friends would join in too if they were there. Lots of drinking though!! The one thing I loved is our family all together, brothers and sister were at one time my sense of security.*

*I also remember one time at band camp... oh no, just kidding, got to have humor in a book right? Anyhow, camping not sure where, my parents like to deer hunt, the one time I do remember was when my cousin Sheri and I got lost in the woods as we wondered off when we were playing, we were about age 4-5, it's funny how certain*

4

*events as young as we were will stick in your mind. Everyone else was out hunting; I am not sure if my mom was sleeping or what, I know she was there when we wondered off, Sheri and I well, we did find our way out and found our camp even as little as we (were).*

*We would always have a fire, I remember the big, fluffy, roasty marshmallows, it was so fun- then bed time came and dad would throw me over his shoulder and down this little hill we went to flat ground where they had all these tents set up for sleeping for us kids. Mom n dad had a camper to sleep in. Anyhow Scary, I remember feeling just scared. Camping was fun; night time was a little creepy, as you could hear wild animals howling. So, you can see, we had some good times as a whole family. But the last memory was me between my mom and dad crying as my mom was leaving my dad this time for good, and my Uncle and Aunt were there to get us.*

*Long story short, my dad resented me later as I started calling my step father, (Dad too.) I was never made to call him Dad; I was the one who asked if I could. My real dad quite asking for me and calling me, I never heard from him much after that. I remember my dad all of the sudden being in the hospital in Idaho, my mom got a call that he had died.*

*We lived in same neighborhood as my Uncle and Aunt; in fact our house was right behind theirs. My mom said run get your Uncle, so I ran to their house and when I realized what I was saying to them I was crushed, and angry, and I - fell to the grown and cried and cried. I would never see him again to be able to tell him I still loved him as my dad. And I never got to say I was sorry for the way he felt about me calling my step father dad, and why I did. My grandmother also had disowned me and I was only a little girl, I didn't understand why the both of them would do such a thing to a little kid, and my own dad. At any rate, I went to his funeral with my older sister and siblings. I was so angry and never told a soul.*

*I hated to cry in front of people, I wanted no one to know how I was really feeling. I really loved my grandma and my real father too. But they did not love me back, so I showed no emotion about that from then on. I cried at my dad's funeral, but from then on if I cried, it was in private or in front of my friend Jill. Jill and I are still friends to this date. We don't always see each other, but when we do, we take off right where we left off. I love her as she will always remain one of my best friends here on this crazy earth.*

*INSECURITY:*

*Back before my Mom re-married and before my real dad died, my mom and dad were divorced or in the middle of one, we lived in an apartment, my mom would often wait till I was a sleep and then she would go out and meet people at the bar. I bet I was 7 or 8. I would often wake up and find her gone and* later she would come home with a different attitude; she smelled like alcohol and cigarettes.  I often felt insecure that she was going to leave and not make it home one day!  One time she came to my school for a conference, well I was there waiting for her, she was late, she showed up reeking of alcohol and cigarettes, at the time (wigs were in style) and her wig was on a bit sideways. She blamed me for not telling her and reminding her of the conference, mind you I was 7 or 8.

 I remember living in an apartment and being bullied at the bus stop.  I told my mom, so she had my older brother go with me to the bus one day to get me off to school, and the kid that was bulling me turned it all on me somehow (I was a quiet kid) and my brother ended up on his side and having a smoke with him, a whole lot of good that did!  At the same bus stop there was a girl by the name of Peggy, she was a little older than me as I was only 7 or 8 at

8

*the time and she asked me if I wanted to play hooky, - well I loved games and said sure - how do you play?  Her reply was - well you act like you're going to school, but you never get on the bus and don't really go to school.  Man, I was all in! (lol).  Sounds fun to me!  We went back home, as we both were in homes that where no one got us off to school, we did it ourselves, soooo who would know!!!  I even made my own lunch for school or I didn't have one. We went back home and ate and played.  Then Peggy came up with another Idea!  She asked me if I wanted to walk to the store and get some candy?  I said sure, but I don't have any money, she said, well you don't need money, I will show you how to get candy without money!  So off we went walking on one of the busiest highways you could ever imagine, (empire way) in Renton.  Walking ourselves to Zippy mart, a small highway grocery owned by a little old man.*

Well we walked right in his store during school hours and came out with boots and pockets full of candy. Peggy showed me the first time and told me that you just make sure no one is looking. Sounded good to me!! So about the third time in his store he caught on to us, after seeing us come in and not buying anything and walking out and during school hours. Well this is about the 7th or 8th day in a row playing hooky and we went into his store and I was so good at this getting candy while no one was looking, and here I was stuffing gum and candy left and right in my boot and that old man was standing right behind me. And he said very loudly WHAT ARE YOU DOING? Stealing from me? He said leave my store and I am calling the police right now! He made sure that our boots and pockets were empty and sent us out. We ran all the way home on that busy highway, while looking behind us to see if the police were after us.

*Although we got caught stealing candy, we still played hooky! Everyday wondering if the police were going to show up at any time and get us. I remember being in the car my mom stopping by the Zippy Mart to get something real quick, and acting like I was a sleep and scrunched down in my seat, so the old man would not see me.*

## *SCHOOL BRINGS OUR AVENTURE TO AN END:*

*Well after two straight weeks of me not showing at school, the school called my mom and asked if Janice had the chicken pocks or something? My mom's reply, well no, why would you ask that? They proceed to say they have not seen her for two weeks so wanted to know what was wrong!!*
*Then I heard, Janice get in here! I was like, oh oh, the police are here! Only to find out they weren't. She asked me what I had been doing the last two weeks (you should have been in school). My reply was very simple (I*

was playing hooky) mom. HOOKY SHE SAID? What in the world she said? Rather loudly may I add....I said it's a game mom, not a big deal! And where did you learn that game she asked, from Peggy, I replied. My friend two doors down. She very loudly explained that is not a game! Those of you that know my mom, you know I am just going to say it, shit hit the fan! My mom says, SO what else have you been doing that she should know about, during those two weeks of not going to school. What in the world have you girls been doing then, she asked? I said very low voiced - playing, eating, watching T.V, stealing candy.....and oh boy! You know what hit the fan again and voices got louder! You've done what? Where? I said the Zippy Mart at the old man store. Oh man! My heart was beating very fast as I told her the police were after me. She marched me out to the car while my brother is laughing, and off we went to the Zippy Mart to see the old man, so I could *apologize. I was saying no! Mom I will go to jail!!! – (lol). Well, she marched me in there and explained what was going on with school and the game I had learned from Peggy, and of course I said, as I was crying, I was sorry!!! Thought for sure I was going to Jail. The little old man accepted my apology and said don't do that ever again as you may just go to jail. This meant he was not sending me to jail, so I was very happy about that. He was a very nice old man; his name was Bill or Bob, something like that. We became buddies; he always gave me a piece of candy each time I went in there to see him after that. He always would ask me how school was. He was like the grandpa that every kid would dream of. A bit grumpy, stern, but very sweet all at the same time. I can still picture him in my mind today.*

## BELIEF DEEP WITHIN:

*My mother was brought up in the church of Nazarene. So she had a mother and father that were believers and so my mom was fed knowledge. What I did not understand is how my mom was often so unhappy. She never really talked about her knowledge much to me; I am not sure about my other siblings. I have 3 brothers and 1 sister and none of them I remember really talking about God at all. I remember my Mom working a lot, and drinking a lot, you know just having fun, but no talk of God! I think maybe because she had to go to church and her parents may have been strong believers and were involved in church and she had no choices, would make sense I guess. I know of other people that ended up rebelling later in life and not continuing to go to church and were confused on what they believed, or used that as an excuse as to why they stopped attending.  Later in my life I figured out that it was more of the relationship with God that matters and that my mom really did have that with God, but for some reason never talked about it till much later, like when she was sober and when she came to live with me. Sometimes I felt my mom did not feel worthy, maybe because of mistakes that were made.  Looking back I think my mom was killing some type of pain with the alcohol.  I was never sure of just what. She did teach us right from wrong and so many other things that were good. I know one time she told me that she still loved my dad, but could not be with him.  When my dad died she cried too as it still hurt her, even though she was remarried.*

*My grandma, my mom's mom; what I remember of her was so beautiful and what I mean by that is her spirit.  I remember as a child seeing her and staying with her a very few times as she lived so far away from us, - I felt secure, lots of love in her home.*

*Looking back now, as an adult, I know now she had an amazing relationship with God. I don't know much about my Grandma Miller, but I did know that about her.*

*DATING:*

*My Mom was dating who later became my step father. At the time I was not sure of his beliefs and as a child really did not care or think of such beliefs or even really know about God at that time. What I did know is that this man in my mom's life, and now in us kid's life, gave me a more secure, stable feeling. My mom could be a handful at times. He brought some stability to her life which helped me feel a bit more stable. I soon would call him dad. I was his little girl. My real father I really never saw too much, as I said before. I am sure it hurt him and he was jealous, it simply got taken out on me.*

*My step father Russ liked to fish and we had a fishing boat that was quite large and fun to spend the night on. He also liked to hunt* pheasant, which is a type of bird that is really good to eat.  He got my mom into both those things along with golf and times were good.  The one thing that was always still involved with those fun things was lots of alcohol.  That never really seemed to go away.  But they were very happy together and had lots of fun, and no one was hitting my mom.    They bought a new house, well it was new to us and was very nice and I had my own bedroom.  This was a surprise to me as the one time I remember going to Idaho to see my dad I came back to a new home and my own room that my mom and step father had all set up for me.  Loved our family dinners- my mom was a wonderful cook. My step father really never had any of his own kids, so I was his little girl!  Well he had a daughter, but really never saw her much till - later in life, she was a lot older like 40's.  I thought that was strange they did not have a relationship till then; it was very sad. And she called him by his first *name; as a kid I did not understand and really to this day I still don't get it.*

*MY BEST FRIEND AND I:*

*So now I am in 6th grade or so and my parents seem stable to me and I am feeling a whole lot more secure. Yeah they still sometimes would be out at the bar but at least I knew that they had each other and I didn't worry as much. Now I had my own things I was getting into and loving life, and wanted to just play with my friends and be with my friends. My best friend Jill and I would ride horses together and that was my thing I liked to do the most is ride horses. My dream was to have my own some day and that is all I talked about. So soon, I got my own horse her name was Angel and she was white. Yes, and guess who got me my horse, yep my step father. This would have been about the time my real father had passed.*

*Jill and I would often hang out with older kids including her sister and we would ride horses till really late at night. We would leave in the morning and not come home till mid night some times. Our parents never knew both sets of parents were both at the bar till late at night on weekends and so we usually would know when we needed to be home so we could beat them home. We thought we were pretty cool, running around in the woods and trails, making camps, and steeling Jill's parent's pots and pans so we could cook soup in the woods around a camp fire. We made a camp out of tarps and rope and used spray paint to color it. Was quite the camp and we had a whole lot of fun.*

*One time we made a tree house camp and stayed all night in it, we would say to our parents that were spending the night at each other's house and would go to the pasture that we got the horses from and stay the night in this tree house we made. We decided to make it more fun by smoking some cigarettes. We thought we were too cool and did not get caught.  We had so much fun and we had more freedom as kids, we thought it was normal and didn't know any different.  We sometimes, back in the day, would trick or treat till mid night going house to house.  Now could you see your child doing that these days? What is more shocking, our parents knew of that one. We did lie quite a few times to our parents as to what we were doing and where.  But they didn't check most of the time, so we were all good.*

*I remember walking in the mud with jeans a tank top and no shoes just bare feet, and us girls with our hair done and make up on!  Of course we often had to put the makeup on in the woods.  Our parents did not like us to wear makeup.  We would often hitchhike to Renton from Skyway.  Now mind you hitch hiking in 6th to 7th grade with my friend's older sister - she was a whole 15 years old. Wow, could you see your kid these days hitch hiking - lol lol - holy cow.  I would shoot my kids if I caught them doing that, oh wait I would probably not have to because now a day's someone else would shoot them.  (Different times for sure).*

*So right about now my girlfriends and I are getting pretty into doing stuff we probably shouldn't be doing.  Like chasing people in the park with a pitch fork dressed up like the devil while on horses.  One time this older lady dropped to her knees and said don't hurt me, not realizing that we were stupid little kids.  I felt awful after that.  We would also smoke pot in the park (don't remember how we even got it). I think that may have been my first time smoking it, if I remember right, I didn't feel all that well after it.  We again like many times were out and about at night time on a weekend, not sure if it was a Friday or Saturday night.  But often were just out and about.  We even sometimes took cigarettes from our moms and dads when they were not looking.  And we were even starting to take a little of the* booze that our parents would have in the cabinet.  We started drinking quite often, looked like fun to us, so we were really getting into it.  I remember throwing up after being dropped off from babysitting going to the side of our house and throwing up like a water fountain. It was awful, but do you think I stopped there?

CHURCH AND IT'S MEANING AS A CHILD:

Every once in a while I would go to church with my cousins, my mother's brother and his kids (plus wife).  I do remember my mom and stepdad going to church every once in a great while, like once a year, maybe twice. Sometimes on Easter, but never do I remember going on Christmas or Christmas Eve, or even around Christmas.  I don't think I really even knew what Christmas even meant.  I knew that sometimes I would hear the term Jesus freaks.  Not sure where, but heard that sometimes. (I think my step father!) I don't even think at that time I *really took the time to understand what it meant.  I thought that it meant a bunch of people that did stuff from the hippy age lol and they were high all the time.  I think there are times I just did not care or pay any attention as to what people were actually saying I would just go along with it and laugh, not really knowing what I was laughing about, and just trying to fit in.*

*Christmas was always my favorite time of the year and still is today!  Back then I did not celebrate the real meaning of Christmas because I really did not know what it all meant.  I knew that Jesus was born in a manger, but that was about what I knew.  My dad (step father) taught me two prayers that were often said at our dinner table.  It was the same prayer over and over and over, do you remember the God is good God is great prayer?  Well that is it; I always thought you had to say a certain prayer with certain words for it to mean anything, for God to hear you.*

*In church I remember when I would go, that there were a lot of words I did not understand, (or maybe did not try to understand) however there were a lot of fancy words, and singing, and lots of crying. There were lots of rules of how you dressed to church. I never heard come as you are; (lol). A lot of it was good I know today, but back then my friend and I would sit in the back and laugh, as some people were funny to us. Then sometimes I would feel bad afterwards for laughing. I even laughed at my own Auntie who would get up in front of the church and sing, and she sang well, not sure why I was laughing, maybe I just did not understand what she was singing, and she during singing would always start to cry.*

*I have a whole side of the family that are very strong Christians. I thank God that they were a part of my life back then. They of course are not perfect, but I am glad they were a part of my life as I needed them and didn't even know it. I must have learned something in that church. It's amazing how we are learning without realizing it. My mom would have my Aunt and Uncle babysit me at times on the weekends and they would take me to church on Sundays. I often would look like Shirley Temple as my cousin would have me sleep like her in curlers, and yep we would be curly. My Aunt would make sure we had a 10 course breakfast before we left for church, so you could imagine we all had to be up bright and early. Pancakes, bacon, eggs, hash browns, orange juice, maybe some donuts (lol)- these people liked to eat, and it was my favorite part.*

*ATTRACTION:*

*It was time for me to start seventh grade, I was so excited. My birthday was in September. When started the 6th grade I had just turned 11, as most kids were 12. So when I was to start 7th grade I was 12. I remember it being a big deal to me and was* a little scared as it was such a big school.  It wasn't really but to someone of that age it seems so.  That year I was starting to have little crushes on boys.  I seemed to like boys that were older than I.  There was one boy I kind of liked, his name was Cam.  Every once in a while I would see him at my friends house hanging out with her brother, but didn't really talk to him, along with others. Also, at school there was a kid that use to play a guitar and entered the talent show, he sang really well for someone so young. It had the words in it Rocking you baba, Rocking you, Rocking you baba.  (Lol) yep that's all I remember about that, so cute tho.  I went away dreaming about him. Lol  I Don't even remember his name.

I was pretty quiet when it came to school, when it came to school work anyway, but could talk and talk to my friends.  There was another kid name Frank I was always trying to impress Frank.  Loved that kid - so cool! Not!  Have you gone out with someone and *then broken up and just wondered what you were thinking?  Yeah, did that a couple times.  Well one time I was in Skyway at this game place, and I was with a couple of friends and these two girls got in a fight outside the place in the parking lot, as in they were having a fist fight, and me and my big mouth decided to cheer the one girl I did know on.  These were not nice girls as I would later find out!*

*My friend's sister and her friend got approached by the girl I was not cheering on to help them get me into a car, to supposedly just scare me, as they did not like that I was cheering the other girl on to win. So my friend's sister and her friend came to my house, my parents were not home, and they said that Frank was out in the car and wanted to talk to me. Of course sooo infatuated with this kid, I hurried and put make up on so I could go with my two friends in this black Monte Carlo to see him, only to find that it was not him at all in the* car, it was this Asian girl and this white girl which at the time had no idea who they were. I had only seen her but one time at the fight she was in. Anyway they proceeded to threaten me and say really odd stuff, and my friend was on one side of me and she was on other side of me and I of course was in the middle and in the back seat. Well the girl turned around from the front seat and proceeded to punch me in the face. When I started to bleed, they started yelling at me, don't get blood all over in my mom's car. I don't even remember if they dropped me back at home or around the block, but somehow I made it home. Even my two friends did not get out with me, they proceeded to go with them. Not sure if they were scared or if they even realized that those two girls had every intention of beating me up. Well the police were contacted and we filed a report but nothing ever happened to any of them. They were a lot older than me as they were licensed to *drive their mom's car.  An older kid beating up younger kids is just not ok.  I think I may have taken it out on some other little kid and should not have done that.  I felt so angry after that, that my two friends would do that to me.  They came and told my mom and dad that they were sorry they didn't know that they were going to beat me up, that they were just suppose to scare me.  Well today I say wow!  The bullying even today has got to stop.*

*Time went on and of course I forgave my two friends, they meant the world to me.*

*I would spend the night at my friend's house and we would do goofy stuff, like dance around to a song called Sugar, Sugar.  And my girlfriends and I would pal around at night here and there and everywhere.  We did have lots of fun.  I remember watching my favorite movie the Wizard of Oz and my girlfriend hiding under the covers as that movie always scared her.  We thought it was* so funny. But she was really frightened of the flying monkeys and the witch. (lol)

**THE NIGHT THAT WOULD CHANGE MY LIFE FOREVER:**

I remember us girls deciding to go out and about as usual and not thinking or having a care in the world. We were in Skyway Park, I, my friend and her sister and someone that my friend's sister knew we were smoking and having fun. Mind you my friend that I was actually with did not smoke at the time and do the stupid stuff that her older sister and I did. She didn't smoke anything that is; although, some of the bratty stuff was mostly her in the park. But for the most part, she just went along with her sister because, well, they were sisters. As for me I just wanted her sister to like me, she was older, and I liked hanging out with her. This was the same one that got me in car when I got beat up. After the park that same night, proceeded to go home as her parents *were gone and they had just made some wine, which was in a garbage can in their kitchen. It was black berry wine or something like that.  I remember us girls decided to help ourselves and drink some of it, was pretty good!  We were singing and dancing and messing around. Having a good old time!  It was me, Jill, Sue and Peggy.*

*Up the drive way came a car with a boy that who had just got his license!  Now you will learn why our laws on teenage driving have changed, due to many things like the experience I am about to tell you.*

*This boy came up the drive way in this car, he was a very nice kid, and us being dingy girls, me being one of them, said let's go for a drive!!  Please Jon take us for a ride. He was real cute, so I thought at the time.  I think then, I thought every boy was cute holy cow!!  So it was me first that said please let's go, so I hopped in middle front seat of course, right next to Jon, then my friend's sister Sue hops in next to me in front on the passenger side and says yeah Jon let's go. Then my friend Jill get's in back and says ok let's go, then my friends sisters friend gets in back and says ok, but I don't think Peggy really wanted to go. Nor do I think Jill really did either.*

*Before you know it were on the road, and singing to music, having a good old time. It was rainy and nasty out though and we probably should not have been in the car with a person that just got their license. Before you know it were headed to Seattle on the freeway. I was a little scared at that time because I didn't want to get in trouble if her parents beat us home and then they would know we were out. But I never said a word. All the sudden we were at Alki Beach. We were on the strip somewhere by Spuds. I remember it just pouring rain out, and I am sleepy. We had turned around from the other end of the strip and were headed back the other way I think to come home, and went around a corner too fast and slid into a big huge tree. I remember just kind of falling asleep and lifting my head as there were screams and seeing this tree and we were going to hit it, and we did. I heard screaming from my friends, and I lifted my head up from the back of the seat and then they stopped yelling like instant as they must have seen all the blood running all over my face.*

*They saw my face and then started to try to help me as my face was covered in blood. I remember Jon saying it's going to be ok and wiping my face. At this time I was feeling very sick to my stomach. And they were just trying to keep me awake until help got there. My heart was pounding and I was just so tired, and felt so sick to my stomach. I must have passed out at that point, the next thing I remember is that I was so cold and wet and on a stretcher and with lights everywhere. I felt rain coming down on me, someone asking to tell them my name, and trying to keep me awake, what's your phone number? And me barely being able to tell them, as I was so tired and wanted to just go back to sleep, feeling sick as blood was running straight to my stomach from my face area down my throat. I don't remember hearing my friends anymore! The rest is history. I don't remember the ride there to Harbor View. Once they got me to the hospital they worked on me just trying to get me stable. I would awake later, after being in a comatose state, feeling pain and more pain. I can't talk by mouth, can't move, my nose I can't breathe, something was in my throat, and every time I would have to swallow it hurt like I was swallowing a small ball. I had tubes coming out my nose, and my head felt like a heavy bowling ball. My leg hurt and would cramp up and I couldn't tell anyone for the longest time. I was in pain and at that time got shots in my arm and in my butt for the pain, not like now days with a drip. I had so many thing running thru my head, like what happened to my friends, were they dead? Did they make it? I hurt so bad I couldn't move my lips.*

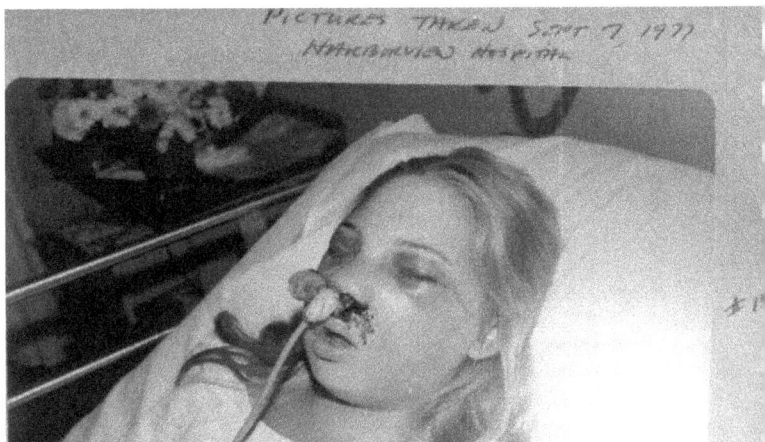

*This picture was taken a couple days after the terrible car accident that I was in and after they washed all the blood out of my hair. I remember hearing the gal that was helping my mom, which was the nurse. My mom and dad had Attorney going to start an investigation to see just what had happened. And they were also taking precaution for insurance reasons. He was going to take pictures of me and I heard my*

mom say please, not with all that blood in her hair.  So the nurse proceeded to hand wash it out while I was in bed.  They were trying so hard to be careful but it hurt so bad, them even touching my head and holding my neck up and all I could do is grunt.  They were finally done!

My body was in so much pain and I learned to grunt and make some noise with my voice like a grunt or a awe sound so they knew I was in pain, they would ask me Janice are you in pain I would try to nod my head yes and grunt.  So here came another shot, but it was worth it!  I just wanted to die, or go to sleep forever.

Before they had washed my hair, and my mom was even there, I heard my step father weeping.  I could not talk to him!  He thought he was just coming to the hospital to just pick me up, they didn't tell him how hurt I really was, or he misunderstood.  He then had to go back to a pay phone to call *my mom, I don't know how but I could hear him speaking to her.  My father told my mom not to come he did not want her to see me like that but of course as a mom does broken arm and all she had my uncle drive her to me at Harbor View in Seattle.  She would not leave me she with broken arm and all spent the night with me until I could wake and make noise, and she knew I was mostly out of the woods.  My mother had just had surgery on her wrist because she had just fallen a few days before my accident at Albertsons parking lot as it was slippery.*

*THE LONG HALL:*

*I had been there in the hospital for quite some time and they were just trying to get the bleeding to stop so they could perform surgery.  My nose was so broken when I came into the hospital my nose was laying down on my face.  My sinuses were shattered along with my cheeks; my cheeks* were so broken they were down hanging by my jaw.  Of course all needed to be fixed.

I remember feeling so hungry but of course No food yet.  Well they got the bleeding to stop it was now then safe enough to do surgery.

The picture on the following page is after they did surgery.  I think I was a sleep for a few days, I don't remember anything but being in pain, and cold freezing skin, which was my face.  I would grunt but I sometimes don't think anyone would hear me.  I am sure they made my mom go home for some rest, as she was there all the time.  In case I would need anything or grunt.  It was so hard because I couldn't tell anyone I was in the type of pain I was in.  Although I am sure that they gave me what they could.  I do remember sleeping most of the time.

I remember wanting to know about my friends, because I noticed they did not come and see me at least I did not hear them.

## WHERE WERE MY FRIENDS?

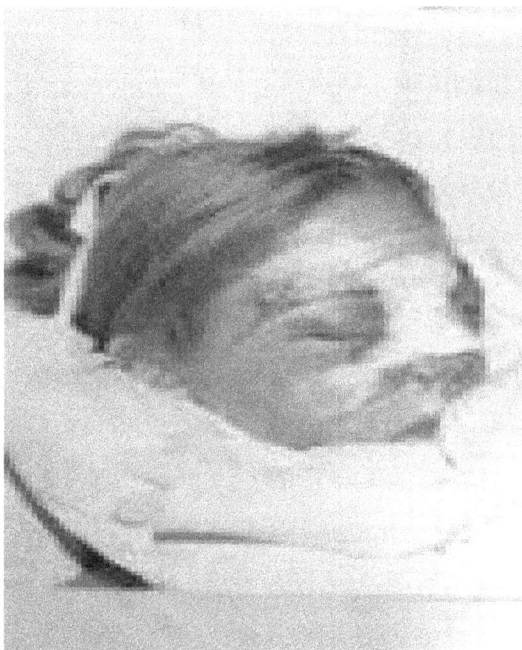

*I didn't realize my friends were not allowed to come see me because I was in intensive care. Seemed like forever! I still could not talk or say what happen to my friends. I had fear that something bad happened to them, as no one even talked about them, around me anyway. I was so afraid that one of them had died; I could not talk at the time*

*so I could not ask. I remember thinking to myself please let them be ok.*

*Days after surgery I was feeling hungry and got to eat jell-o, broth. It was so good. I could barely open my mouth but with someone feeding me I could eat a little at a time.*

*I still was feeling the small ball in my throat and was whispering take it out, take it out. It hurts my throat! I would say that till someone would hear me. I finally heard not yet honey but soon. At this time I could barely open my eyes, just peeking through my eyelashes. My eyes were still so crusted shut. It was time for another surgery for what I am not sure to this day but I had had a few.*

*Oh good time to take the tubes out of my throat, that little ball was being taken out, but they did it in my room, and up it came into my mouth and out it had to come thru my jaws, which meant I had to open my mouth, oh it hurt so bad they had a hard time me opening my mouth to get it out. I felt like I was not getting air and felt scared again. Finally I open my mouth just enough for them to just get it out.*

*Another surgery my mouth was to be wired n rubber band shut so I could not open my mouth anymore. This was so my loose teeth would hopefully adhere to my gums again and my cheeks would not move. They had already gone thru my temples to do plastic surgery for my cheeks, that's what you see at my temples. After many days now I am feeling a little better and can have liquids, runny potatoes n gravy, milk shake, yum. At the time was so good.*

## MY FIRST COUPLE OF DAYS OUT OF BED!

*I so wanted to see what I looked like as I had not seen myself yet. I was sitting in my chair in my room, I was still in intensive care at this point, but had walked to the bathroom with the nurse and she had sat me back down in my chair. I was seeing three's and fours at that time, but wanted to see myself. So I got myself up and walked over slowly with my ivy's and got to the mirror. I wanted to see my face not really knowing what to expect. I remember wanting to though and was going to get to that mirror or in my case the three mirrors I saw. I finally got over there and looked to see that I looked like Frankenstein. I was horrified at*

*what I saw. About then I got caught by the nurse and she helped me back to my bed. And of course she said not to do that yet by myself as I could get hurt. Anyway I just wanted to die after seeing myself. I was up high in the building stories up and thought how it would be to jump out that window. With my luck I wouldn't die and be in more pain. I was more or less feeling very sorry for myself.*

*I believe shortly after that my mom's friend Eddie who was my mom's best friend came in with this huge donkey with a pink ribbon, I was so excited about that little surprise. I named it JACKSON. He was so important to me when I felt sad I just looked at him and that stuffed animal brought me more joy as the days went on. I would tell him my secrets I had in my mind. I had deep secrets I dare not to tell anyone.*

## TIME FOR ME TO LEAVE INTENSIVE CARE:

*Well things were going better but still did not get to go home. Instead I got to go to a different floor. At first they put me on a floor with other teenager's with behavior problems. And I had a new roommate!!! Oh boy lucky me! My mom had bought me a milk shake and brought it to me when I was moving and the new roommate just when I moved in said to me I will take a drink of that and took it from me, took a drink and then tried to give it back to me. I looked at my mom with fear and said I don't want it back. And I want out of here!!! That girl was so disturbed I would be afraid to go to sleep as I was scared of her, and she would hurt me. So they moved me to another room, and different floor.*

*I had a room to myself at first but then another room mate was moving in, she had been in a bad car accident too. She had just come back from surgery and could tell she was in pain too. Later to find out they were a Christian family that lived near me in Sky way her name was Michelle. After she got a little better she and I would watch T.V or at least I would try to watch T.V. it was hard still as I saw a few T.V.'s. She was a very nice girl.*

*I remember being in pain one night and me begging the nurse not to give me another shot as she was instructed to do so and was on time limit. But my Butt hurt so much and my arms that she said ok, let's try to crush up a pill, but because my mouth was rubber band shut now, I could open barely. So the nurse crushed up a pill and put in some water and proceeded to try to pour in my mouth with me starting to wave my arms to get her to stop as it was making me sick she proceeded anyway and I with rubber band jaw began to throw up all over her n my bed. It was awful! I felt terrible as she was trying to give me an alternative to the shot,*

she had a mess to clean up instead.
Needless to say I took the shot from then on.

Now I am only seeing in two's so my vision is getting better.  I was told I may get to go home in a few days.  Believe it or not I was scared to go home, because I did not want to sleep in my bed at home by myself.

My whole family smoked and I was coming home and could not be around smoke, so Dr. did tell them not to smoke around me at all. That they should go outside. Well that worked for awhile.

Well here comes the day I was getting released and was time to go home.  Michelle had already gone home I think at that time. So after one month of being in Harbor View I was to go home.

My brother Dan drove my mom to get me. My mom still had her arm in a cast.  I remember being on the road on I-5 and seeing too many cars for my liking so I laid *my head back.  That brought back memories so I raised my head and just closed my eyes. The Dr. said I may have flash backs on the way home, I did a little, scared but ok.  My mom would ask over and over are you ok honey?  I would say yes just because I didn't want her to worry but I was really scared. When we got home I went directly to the couch.  That would be my bed for a while till I was ok sleeping in my own bed.*

*Lots of people would come to see me in the hospital and even my friend Jill at one time got to come see me so was nice to know she was ok.  But now I was home and she could come to my house so I could see her and I couldn't do much for a while but she still came just to sit with me and watch T.V.  I was still seeing double then but if I just closed one eye I would just see one T.V. and not two and sometimes three.*

## WHAT HAPPENED TO EVERYONE ELSE IN THE ACCIDENT?

*I learned while I was in the hospital that everyone was ok and just waiting for me to come home. I learned something kind of odd, we all got hurt in the order we got into that car to go for a joy ride. I got hurt the worse, my friends sister got a broken Jaw, my friend Jill got two gashes on both her legs, and my friends sister's friend was not hurt but a bump on her head. The boy that was driving ended up with a gash on his head.*

*We had been in a car with not only with someone that just got their license but with someone that was driving a car with bald tires. He was a very nice person and felt so bad, as he took fault. Yes, he should not have driven us, but us girls had no business in his car and we knew better and knew we should have not left that home that night.*

*So, do I blame him or have I ever blamed him? No, we were all at fault.*

*It took a while before my mom and dad would let me go anywhere, as you could imagine.  So I was at home a lot.  Just trying to get well and I slept a lot.  I often thought of my secret I was holding inside.  And just didn't feel comfortable talking to anyone about what I knew!  Things that happened to me!  Thinking people would put me in a strait jacket if I told anyone what I had experienced.*

*I WAS SO HUNGERY AT TIMES:*

*So many times my mom would put pizza in a blender just so I could taste real food. Lol or a roast and mash potatoes so I could slurp it up through a straw, everything I could get threw that straw I did.  She took such good care of me. And I was thankful.*

*Well it was about two months later and time for another surgery it was time to go back to* the hospital to have all the rubber bands, and brace that was holding my cheeks and teeth in place, it all kept me together while I healed, all of it had to come out.  After my surgery was time to be tutored by a home school teacher as I had forgot everything, math, spelling all of it.

After my last surgery I was ready to eat a good meal.  Mom stopped at McDonalds on the way home and I munched down my first burger in months.  Not sure how many months had gone by at this point.  All I know is that at Christmas time I still had the little steal things in my temple that made me look like Frankenstein.  I was so glad they were to be gone.

As time went on I would look in the Mirror and wonder why I am still here.  I looked so bad; I had scars where my nose was put back together and scars on my upper nose bridge where glasses would go, and on each side.  I had scars on my eyebrows, over and *under my eyelids. I still looked so scared up and often wondered if the scars would ever really fade.  At the same time I would still think of my secret, and wondered why I chose to stay, because I was so ugly.*

*MY SECRET COULD NEVER COME OUT:*

*I would often think and pray!  I had a new relationship, that I was terrified to tell anyone about.  As I did not want anyone to think that I was crazy.  No one ever told me anything or even discussed the accident.  I was not sure why, were they protecting me from something?*

*See I knew that I had died and they were not telling me or did they even know? (Well I knew but never said a thing.)*

*I remember everything, in that operating room where they were trying to save me, I saw myself from above in there while they were working on me.  And remember wondering what am I doing down there and*

*I am up here? I felt cold, but no pain, I felt free but was wondering what next what do I do? Where am I? I then was pulled and things went dark!! I did not see this big bright light as others have talked about. It was not that way for me, it was more of feeling a bit lost for a bit, no pain but lost. Flowing, floating, in the dark. Before I knew it I was kneeling before who I would call God and two others. God was in the middle and there was someone on each side of him, one of them I would say may have been Jesus, the other I am not sure of whom it was.*

*I have tried to find a picture of an older wise figure of whom I was before, but have not seen one close enough to put in my book.*

*I remember conversing with God without our lips moving, like the picture below.*

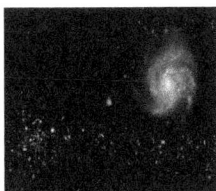

*It seemed so long in*

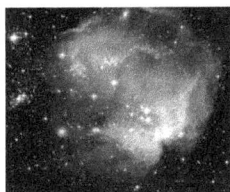

*time*     *tunnel like*

*talking without our lips moving, feeling grace, and peace, love.*

*This would be my new relationship I was talking of earlier and the secret I was going to keep to myself. I would be different forever from now on. I remember him speaking to me. And I don't remember all that he exactly said to me but I do remember kindness, love and saying to him and begging him to go back that I was not done. And could I please go back to my parents that I would be good and do better my life. At that point I remember putting my head down as I was kneeling and put my head down and closed my eyes, and said over and over (please) my father, I believe I was crying. I know many things were said to me by him. Before I knew it I was in a lot of pain. Wishing now I would have just stayed with him.*

*I made the choice not to tell anyone not even my parents. I think I may have told my friend Jill later that I thought I had died, but didn't tell her much more as I think she was unsure how to feel about it.*

*I have had an amazing relationship with God ever since. Not that I held my end of the deal. I still did things that were not what I should have done. I in no way ended up being perfect by any means. In fact more lessons were to come. Lol*

*There was something special about me now though I can still feel it today. My relationship was (and is) amazing because of the things I had already experienced. It was no doubt that I had met the higher power and our creator, who we call God, our Lord, and our King. I can still to this day picture him plain as day. I have since then been trying to find an image that is close so I can share it with people some day!!*

*TIME TO SHARE WHAT I KNEW WITH MY STEP FATHER:*

*Now I am older, and my step father has had a couple surgeries. He kept having blockage in his neck and would have to take veins from his leg and have them put in his neck. I was still young. My step father tried to stop smoking many times but just never did. They became heavier drinkers even. My dad retired and my mom was still working as they were like 10 or so years apart in age. So he did retire before her.*

Instead of doing the things that he should have been doing he would sit home and have drinks even in his coffee, sometimes he would go do some stuff to keep him busy. But he usually would wait for my mom to come home from work, but she would not always come right home she would stop at cheers in Renton.  So of course he would go meet her.  And of course they would drink.

My dad/step father was in pain sometimes in his legs. His circulation was getting bad.  I was now married and had two children.  A lot was going on at the old house, of course with a lot of smoking and drinking.  My dad I know would get upset that my mom would end up at the bar and then he would have to go fish her out, he would say to me when I would come over.  My dad was just not doing very good at that time and was told by the Dr. that he may have to have his leg amputated if they couldn't get his circulation working better.

*One day I went over to my mom and dad's house only to find that my dad was at the kitchen table, and kind of upset. He was telling me that he did not want his leg amputated and did not really want to live that way. That he was also kind of scared because he had an aneurism and was afraid of dying, you could tell he was disturbed.*

*Well I was older now and I was about to tell him about me dying and that it was ok. And share my experience with him. But before I could get it out he said to me, you know honey I never told you and should tell you that you died when you got in that car accident when you were younger, you had died they said for 1 minute when they were working on you in the operating room. They almost lost you. I started to cry and said Dad I know!!! That is what I was just about to tell you, about that very thing! Although I did not know how long I had died for that part was now a little clearer.*

*I now have my dad in tears! I was letting him know that dying does not hurt and is not something to be afraid of. Letting him know of my relationship I had been building since I had died. Sharing with him that God is Real dad, and you can depend on him and trust him. You just have to believe in him, and pray to him talk to him, no fancy words, just your words. He will listen to you! You need to save yourself by loving your father, your creator! He loves you dad just like he loves me. He was so shocked in what I was in fact telling him, I shared with him everything I knew from A to Z from the time I was in the accident to the time I was looking down on the table that I was being worked on in the hospital when the Dr.'s were trying to save me. I shared the black dark like place, to the beauty that I kneeled before and asked for forgiveness and begged to come back. I said over and over to him Dad, God is Real!! GOD IS REAL!*

*I left him and he was feeling a little better you could tell.  I believe that his relationship with God started that day!*

*THE CALL I WAS NOT EXPECTING:*

*I am a full time Real Estate Agent and was out showing many homes that year, I had made a choice not to put my children in day care and one day my husband came home and found that I quit my job, that I thought may become my career.  But I was not going to be away from my daughter that long any more as my commute was an hour. So I went out the next couple days and found a Job close to home. My new job was at a Real Estate firm, I was the new secretary in fact it was the first job I had tried to get and was only 5 minutes from home.  It was perfect.  I soon then became a Realtor.*

*I was out showing a home to my friend Jill's mother and father in- law, and we had looked at a few homes, we were hungry so we went to burger King, and I had one of*

59

*those new cell phones that were the size of a brick lol.  We were in the middle of the line and I got a call from my brother in-law and when I heard his voice thought right away that it was odd that he was calling me as he usually didn't.  He said to me that I need to come to his house right away.  And I asked why that I was in the middle of showing homes.  He said that I still needed to go drop them off and come to his house now!  So I said bull shit, (something my mom always said lol) tell me what the hell is going on and now!!! See not very good language see still just not perfect lol. What is wrong?  I first thought something was wrong with my husband or Children or something.  So he went ahead and just told me that my dad had passed a couple of hours ago. Poor Jill's in-laws had a ride they will never forget.*

*Leaving and not picking up food we had all ordered over the barrier then over the divider to take them to their car, I said I had to go get out my dad just died.  They of course were very understanding, a little scared of my driving skills at the time....Will never forget their eyes were so bold they could have popped right out. lol still can see in my head today! lol I can laugh today, but at the time they may have thought I was a bit off my rocker. (As my mom would always say).*

*My dad had died in his sleep, it was said that his aneurism had exploded in his sleep. Of course I was very upset!! But knew that he was where he was so scared of going, at first that is until we talked just two weeks before he died. He had said to me that day that he wanted to die in his sleep. I believe he not only started that huge relationship with our Father God, but he also was brave enough to ask him if he could just come home as he did not want to have his leg gone, and live that way. I can see him now asking God and can I just please come home and when I do, can I go in my sleep and in peace? I see my dad saying that very thing to God as he was* talking about it that day I and he shared about my dying for that minute.  By the way that minute seem so long in what I believe was heaven.  I know that there was brightness once I was thru the darkness, and know that it was so amazing.  I also know that some of what God and I talked about I don't remember and some of the scenery,  I may not be able to describe it to a tee, I believe that God may not want me to tell you everything as it would spoil some of the surprise he has in store or you, and your experience with him.

I so remember conversing without moving our lips and speaking out loud.  I remember such an amazing feeling of rest, peace, grace, love, comfort, I also remember no fear.  But do remember feeling a loyalty and a sternness, but forgiveness.  I was his child! I was his daughter!  I would never be lost again, if I need something all I have to do is ask, it may be in God's timing but so many things I have asked for today is here right *now!! I never used fancy words, just my true feelings when having my time with my God, my King, my father, my creator.*

*Now I know my dad had his experience with God and was probably very unique and just for him. I bet it was amazing and he would not choose to come back here. I was so excited for him as we just had talked of the great things that could happen for him if he just asked. I was very sad too and missed him so much. He was my father here on earth, he was my security at one time, he was who I had as my male figure, he is who showed me how women should be treated as he treated my mom like gold. He loved her so much. I loved him so much; it was so hard to let him go, but knew he was ok.*

*MISTAKES:*

*Now did I get to go thru my life without any mistakes or lessons and was I perfect, nope I would have to endure lessons just like everyone else here on earth. Learn and*

Learn, and try not to make the same mistakes over and over. God changed my life. Do I need God every day still? YES, I would have to ask him for guidance, where he wanted me to be next, or forgive me for I had sinned, or share feelings I did not know what to do with. Prayers and keeping track of what I prayed for and watch how my prayer would come alive, letting me know and giving me the faith that he is still there. This, my dear friend (reader), happens all the time. The confirmation of praying today and watching God work in my life and others as I have prayed. It is amazing.

RELATIONSHIP:

You see all you have to do reader is believe, talk to him, and love him as he loves you. Write down what you pray about too, so you don't miss his answer. Before you know it you will not always need to write down as you will become very good at recognizing his answers when they arrive. Your relationship *will grow and grow.  Now, he may not always give you exactly what YOU want, not always but he will answer.  He makes you want him depend on him thru life lessons, so learn apply what you learn.  Don't use your parent's mistakes as an excuse to fail. We all as parents are not perfect. Give thanks for your lessons; give thanks everyday even when you're feeling you're having a bad day.  Smile a lot, laugh a lot even if you don't really feel like it, it's very healthy! Don't forget that God has a sense of humor so share your fun and good times with him. Don't just share your worries and times of need of him in sad situations, don't get me wrong you should always ask him for help and share those times of needs, but it's ok to share your dreams and blessings you may want in your life, share with him when you are happy and a funny joke, or even just staring at a beautiful bird or mountain and tell him thanks my father for such beauty. Or maybe just a great day you had and in* the middle of it say God are you there? I know you are because I feel your warmth and thank him for that feeling you just had and know that is him. Include him when it's wonderful or even if it is icky ice-cream laugh and include him. If you see someone having a bad day or homeless, say God bless this situation somehow my father, or someone that needs healing, just a few words to your father in heaven, say I don't know all about this situation father but you do and I trust you father. Give our father your full trust and know His plan is always perfect. Perfect with you in mind, you are his child. Remember to take care of what God gives you.

Forgive often, as God has forgiven you, he will if you ask him. God's plan is forever perfect. GOD IS REAL!

I am not a professional writer I am just me!

Janice Laree Geary